HARD CHOICES, EASY DECISIONS

Mary Alice Kellogg

A FIRESIDE BOOK
PUBLISHED BY SIMON & SCHUSTER
New York · London · Toronto · Sydney · Tokyo · Singapore

Fireside

Simon & Schuster Building
Rockefeller Center
1230 Avenue of the Americas
New York, New York 10020

DESIGNED BY DIANE STEVENSON/SNAP-HAUS GRAPHICS

Manufactured in the United States of America

1   3   5   7   9   10   8   6   4   2   Pbk.

Library of Congress Cataloging in Publication Data

Kellogg, Mary Alice.
    Hard choices, easy decisions / Mary Alice Kellogg.
    p.   cm.
    1. Decision-making.   I. Title.
BF448.K45   1991
153.8'3—dc20   90-21652
                                                      CIP

ISBN 0-671-67282-7 Pbk.

●

For Paul Scanlon and
Samantha Wishman

• ACKNOWLEDGMENTS •

A few very special people were invaluable in making this system and this book a reality, so knowing whom to thank is an easy decision for me.

Foremost, my deepest gratitude to Seymour Wishman, the best decision maker I know. Without his insight, vision, common sense, and good humor every step of the way, this book would not have been possible. Many thanks also go to my agent Elaine Markson, for her enthusiasm and belief in the project, and for her friendship.

For her interest and early guidance, special appreciation to Laura Yorke at Simon & Schuster. And last, but by no means least, Senior Editor Ed Walters at Fireside deserves a round of applause for his focused and professional editorial cyc. Working with him made publishing, always a collaborative effort, a pleasure.

HARD CHOICES, EASY DECISIONS

• THE DECISION DILEMMA •

Let's start with a very simple quiz. Which would you rather do—make a major decision or have root canal work done by your dentist?

If you're like most Americans, the unhappy prospect of the dentist wins easily. Why? Because the physical pain we experience in the dentist's chair is nothing compared to the mental anguish, frayed nerves, fingernail-chomping anxiety most of us associate with having to consider options, weigh them, and then choose.

Decision making has become one of our society's least-favorite things to do. We look upon someone who whips off important decisions with great dispatch and confidence as the ancient Greeks looked upon their many gods. How do they *do* it? We seem to live in an age where indecisiveness creeps into our daily lives like a nasty little virus that has no cure. We want to throw up our hands and give into the sweet, numbing paralysis of just not deciding at all.

How did we become willing victims for the indecisiveness virus? For one thing, we live in a time of staggering choice. Technology, changing social mores, education, a longer life span, new ways of looking at work, new economic resources, and, through the media, information overload—all have given us hundreds, thousands of possible avenues to follow. There are options all over the place, options that our ancestors and even our parents never dreamed of in their lifetimes.

In another, different age, lives were almost completely prescribed. Depending on your social and economic status, the decisions regarding career, marriage, and childbearing were determined for you by family and society. You dressed just so. You behaved just so. You mostly spoke and associated with those who were just like you. Women had their "proper" role to play, and so did men. There was little deviation from the rules; any departure was swiftly punished.

A friend of mine often sighs for the "The good old days, when there weren't so many choices available and so many decisions to make. You could just *be*."

She's kidding, of course. Knowing her, if she did live in the good old days, she'd be fighting hard against the social constrictions of the times. But we all know what she means. Another friend, a man, longs for the good old days, too, when women weren't so . . . complicated. "A sweet, old-fashioned girl is what I need," he sighs. And then he thinks twice. If he had this old-fashioned girl, she would, true to type, look to him for guidance in everything. In short, he'd be stuck making *all* the decisions. And that's a thought that makes him shudder. Make all the decisions? No thanks! He'll take his chances with today's newfangled working woman.

Perhaps more than any other time in history, we are confronted almost daily with decisions that need resolution. And unlike in the past, when the constrictions were clear cut, the rules have changed. Contemporary life is not a matter of everything being black or white: gray is the color of the day, and there are both redeeming and damning facets to just about everything.

Now that society has changed, it's no longer making our important decisions for us. Increasingly we have to find our own way—always a difficult proposition. Making a decision is our responsibility alone, and that responsibility often weighs heavily in a time when so many options are available. It can be paralyzing viewing the number of choices we have. No wonder nostalgia is big business in the United States; we are convinced that yesterday, when we were younger and seemingly had fewer decisions to make, was the best time of all. Life was so . . . simple then, wasn't it? The decisions that we did make didn't seem to be so very important, did they?

● THE DECISION TRAP ●

Of course we're nostalgic. Who can blame us? As children, we're given very little responsibility. Our decisions are simple ones—whether or not to eat the mystery lunch dish in the school cafeteria, who is going to be our "best, best friend" this week. After grade school, things begin to get difficult. The social morass of high school, choosing a college, moving away from home for the first time—we're faced with more and more decisions, building in complexity.

As we grow older, the decisions we make take on increasing importance. There's more at stake than what to eat or what movie to see or what major to choose. Things are more complicated. Should I take a new job? Move to a new city? Buy or rent? Get married? Have a child? Add those to the countless decisions we make every day—what to wear, what telephone calls to return, whether to stay at home and beat the flu or get out of bed and go to work, what highway to take to get to grandmother's house—and the possibilities become staggering.

Naturally, we're exhausted. Of course we're stressed. And it's a competitive world out there, increasingly so. In such an atmosphere, the consequences of making any decision are magnified.

Fear is part of the territory. And it is also the biggest block to making a good decision. Fear begins as a nagging little thought in the back of our heads as a decision looms, then often builds to screaming ogre proportions as we are forced to face that decision. We fall, simply, into the Decision Trap.

The Decision Trap is an easy place to get stuck. How do I know I'm making the right decision? What if I make a mistake? What if I look stupid or ugly or wimpy as a result of my decision? What if I make the wrong one and someone is hurt? What if something terrible happens as a result of a decision I made? What if things are never, ever the same again because of me? What if I ruin my life/my children's lives/the planet as a result of a bad decision? These kinds of questions, exaggerated or not, pop up to haunt us and, in the process, increase our chances of making a bad decision. Fear gets us by the throat and becomes a self-fulfilling prophecy.

This happens because we think that we must be perfect when we make a decision. We flog ourselves, insisting that we must know every single option and consequence, and its ultimate effect on everybody, before we make a final decision. No wonder root canal work seems like a breeze in comparison!

In truth, no mere mortal can know all the above. As countless people will tell us during our lifetimes, nobody is perfect. Believe these people, for nobody is.

So when a decision looms the first thing we do is set ourselves up for paralysis, for disappointment, for dire unforeseen consequences. Who wants to make a decision under these conditions? Not I. And not you.

The way out of this Decision Trap is, like most good things, a simple one. When fear grabs you by the throat and begins to squeeze, think of what a good decision maker you are. Yes, *you*. You make hundreds of decisions, of varying size, every day. And the planet still spins. You decide when to get up, what toothpaste to use, whether to grow a beard or shave, when to take in the dry cleaning, whether to drink coffee or tea, whether to get on the crowded bus or wait for a less crowded one in another five minutes, what radio station to play in your car.

But these are simple, even silly decisions, you might say, decisions made without thinking. What's more, they're not even *decisions*. They're something else, something that doesn't count. We think a decision must begin with a capital "D" and involve some kind of anguished, life-or-death issue in order to be worthy of the term.

Well, think again. The truth is that all those decisions you take for granted prove that you are very good at decision making. Otherwise you couldn't get out of bed in the morning and continue your day. "They're not really decisions," you might say. Wrong. Each and every one is a decision, and we tend to lose track of that. In the process, we forget to stop for a second and pat ourselves on the back for making all those decisions that get us through a day. As a result, we don't see ourselves as decision makers when in reality every single person who is able to function out in the world *is* a decision maker. Not necessarily a Greek-deity type, but a decision maker nonetheless. And that is something to be proud of. Take a bow, for you deserve it.

Usually, we make decisions with confidence or maybe just a little thought. We don't agonize, tear out our hair, or snarl at the cat when we make them. None are the kind of decisions that would change the course of history. Put together, however, they form the fabric of our daily lives. Yet we still persist in thinking of decisions as something to dread and be feared rather than what they are: friendly tools for getting through, moving forward, making life a bit better.

Thinking back on all the decisions you make, you'll notice that you might have made some mistakes along the way. Perhaps you chose the wrong tie or the wrong blouse for that business meeting. Perhaps you shouldn't have ordered that kitchen gizmo advertised on late-night television. Maybe white was the wrong color to paint the kitchen table. Maybe you should have found out before you bought tickets for the X-rated movie that your blind date was a former nun. Perhaps putting that lamp shade on your head wasn't the best way to thank your host for a lovely party.

Mistakes all, sure. Unfortunate decisions, too. But some you can laugh about. You learned from others. When you think of it, all these messed-up decisions probably helped you to make better decisions down the road. And hardly any of these mistakes changed the course of your life or ruined you forever.

In fact, it's impossible to be sure what the consequences of our decisions—"good" or "bad"—will be.

Maybe the ex-nun was offended at the X-rated movie and vowed never to see you again. But there's also the possibility that she was charmed by your obvious embarrassment, and the situation gave you two a chance to laugh and open up a channel of communication that wouldn't have been there if you had gone to see *Snow White*. Maybe the kitchen gadget was a dud and a waste of money. However, it's also possible that your attempts to try to make it work resulted in a funny story for your friends. Putting the lamp shade on your head was embarrassing, to say the least. But maybe there was a talent scout at the party and your antics could lead to a career as a comedian.

You can never know every single consequence. It's impossible to predict. So breathe easy.

There are several factors that hold us back from making decisions, and from looking at decision making as a friendly instead of a hostile process. As we've seen, the feeling that we must be perfect and able to anticipate every consequence plays a role, as do the times in which we live. Thinking we're simply not good at making decisions, the fear of making a mistake—these also contribute to the Decision Trap.

One of the worst factors creating decision anxiety

is the feeling that once we make a decision, it is set in stone forever. A decision may seem irrevocable. We must stay with it, no matter what the consequences. If we don't stick with it, (1) a large bolt of lightning will come down and strike us and our loved ones dead; (2) our loved ones—or even our unloved ones—will hate us or think we are jerks; (3) we will have lost a onetime opportunity to transform our lives into a heaven on earth; (4) we will step off a cliff into an abyss without a ladder; or (5) everything we hold dear will shrivel up and disappear. Silly, perhaps, but fear does have a way of blowing things up all out of proportion.

In fact, there are few decisions that are so irrevocable that we can't go back and take another course. The opposite of the small decisions we unthinkingly make every day is the Big Decision that traditionally creates anxiety. But think about it for a moment. Serious as the potential decision may be, your capacity for ruining your life or the lives of others is pretty slim.

There are some irreversible decisions, of course, decisions that should provoke large doses of anxiety. Deciding whether to press a red button and launch a global thermonuclear war, thereby blasting the planet to pieces, is one. So is homicide. But it's not likely that you'll ever be in the position to have to decide "yes" or "no" on either. Beyond that, just about any decision you make will have some good points for and some good points against, and, whatever you decide, something good will result. Rest easy: if worse does come to worst, you can make another decision to change it.

Sometimes it's not the decision itself that is difficult for us to make, but the idea that, once made, we're wedded to that decision for life, no matter what factors pop up subsequently. What this syndrome fails to take into consideration is the fact that life is in a state of constant change, even the most seemingly uneventful life. Our moods change. Our perspectives change. Our priorities change. We are not shackled to any decision forever simply because we made that decision; if anything, we have the responsibility to evaluate our decisions along the way and change the ones that aren't working. Such a course of action is not running away, it's the opposite. We show we can stick around and be involved. Changing our minds doesn't necessarily mean that we're not committed; it can show just the opposite.

WHY OTHER METHODS DON'T WORK

Now that you feel better about making decisions in general, and perhaps have a few in particular to make coming up, what's the best way to make one? Assuming you've taken a deep breath, given it a lot of thought, and vanquished the fear monster that has been strangling you with anxiety, you're facing yet another obstacle before you can make that decision freely and with a less heavy heart. Yes, you have to wade through the Valley of the Methods.

The Valley of the Methods is populated by old, well-meaning friends whom you're sure to recognize. There are three in particular who are brought up time and time again. If they seem familiar, it's because they're the most often touted as a decision maker's dream. They're dragged out every time there's a major decision to be made, whenever the first stab of anxiety hits, or the first fingernail is bitten down on in anticipation. And, almost as swiftly, they get put back on the shelf as a serious case of decision paralysis sets in. These methods may be old friends, but these old friends simply don't work. Let's take them one at a time to discover why.

• LISTING PROS AND CONS •

"Do whatever *you* think is best." How many times do we hear this concerning a big decision, and from how many people? But how do you know what is best? Chances are, the helpful friends and relatives who tell you to do what you think is best will also tell you to make a list of the pros and cons as a time-proven way to help your decision along.

At first glance, this method seems to make a lot of sense, for aside from some obvious decisions—like whether to push the red button or hire Vinnie the hit man—it's not always immediately clear which choice is the best. Often we don't know what we really want; and we need to take a deep breath and consider the factors that might have an impact on our decision. What better way to do this than to list, in one column, all the factors in favor of your decision and, in another, the factors against?

So you take a legal pad and draw a line down the

center. Let's say the decision you need to make is whether to take a vacation to the Grand Canyon in the summer (instead of in the autumn, for example). You think a bit, and end up with a sheet of paper that looks like this:

• GRAND CANYON SUMMER VACATION •

PROS	CONS
More Lively Crowd	More Expensive
More Going on	Hot Drive
Great Sunsets	Evening Thunderstorms
Better Service	Mosquitoes
More Social Life	More Families Traveling

What you end up with is a nice little list of summer vacation joys and hazards. Within the list are some pros (more activities, great sunsets) and some cons (hot drive, mosquitoes).

But you also end up with a bunch of other things. "More families traveling" could be a con if you didn't want to be around small children, or a real advantage if you had a family of your own. "More lively crowd" could be an asset if you're a young couple looking for an active night life, or a real drag if you're looking for peace and quiet. And for some, "mosquitoes" are merely a summer nuisance; others are violently allergic to their bites.

As you go down your list of what's good and what's not, you begin to discover why this method sounds good in theory but is troublesome in practice. While good and bad points can be listed, there is no way to weigh each one as to its relative importance to *you*. The result is usually a list where the "pros" and the "cons" are identical in number—five good reasons to do something and five good reasons not to. When each factor is given equal weight, you haven't reached a decision, but a standstill. Making a list of the pros and cons may be a good way to discover some of your thoughts and priorities, but it is only a start in the decision-making process. It cannot truly help you to decide.

ASKING THE OPINIONS OF OTHERS

No one lives in a void. Each and every one of us is influenced by other people, starting with our parents and family, then our siblings, peers, friends, spouse, boss, co-workers. Just about anyone we come in contact with leaves some kind of imprint upon us, which is not a bad thing in and of itself. Nor is taking into consideration the thoughts and opinions of others.

When faced with a perplexing decision, the urge to turn to a respected friend and ask, "What would *you* do in this situation?" is a strong one. It is also a natural reaction, for often hearing someone else's thoughts on a situation will help you to more clearly put your own thoughts into perspective.

However, when the opinion of other people becomes the *most important* influence on a key decision you're making, even bigger problems can develop. Permitting others to unduly influence your decisions is an abdication of responsibility. Certainly life would be easier, we think, if somebody else made all the decisions . . . but we know in practice that path can lead to frustration, confusion, and, ultimately, unhappiness.

Putting too much stock in what others say you should do can be pretty confusing, especially if the decision is a more complex one (it's easier to ask a friend if you should wear the stripe or the paisley than to ask "Should I marry Bob?"). What if several people you respect each have a different idea of what your next move should be? At its best, listening to too many voices can cloud your own judgment. At its worst, this method puts you at risk of putting too much power into the hands of others, of being manipulated.

Let's say, for instance, you have an offer for a better job at another company. You ask your best friend, who just happens to work at the next desk, what you should do. If your friend is secure, she might tell you to go for it, to seize the opportunity for advancement. But she could also advise against your leaving, either because she (1) will miss you at work and wants you to stay or (2) is concerned that this new job will place you too far ahead of her in the career track and will lead to your friendship becoming strained, perhaps even ending your friendship in the process.

In the former case, your friend wishes you well and advises you to leave based on what she thinks you can accomplish elsewhere. In the latter case, she's advising you to make a decision, not on the basis of what's good for you, but what's good for *her*. In neither case, however, is she making a decision based on what might truly be best for you. Even the most altruistic of motives can muddle your thoughts when decision time comes. And there's even a third possibility regarding your friend's advice: with the best of intentions, her judgment could be simply wrong.

While listening to the opinions of those we respect and love is a valuable and even desirable part of living, if we place too much value on their ideas of what our own actions should be, we could be laying the groundwork for real decision-making disaster. It's good to listen to others when making a decision—they may suggest more pros and cons than we had originally considered. But, as we will soon see, it's even better to listen to ourselves in weighing what's important to us.

• LISTENING TO EXPERTS •

 W e live in a world that has no shortage of experts telling us how to achieve success, happiness, and love. The pages of magazines and newspapers and countless books are filled with advice on how to have thin thighs and fat bank accounts. On radio and television authorities tell us how to dress right, when we're eating wrong, the correct reasons to marry, the best way to raise children, and the worst way to fire an employee. While well meaning, such an overabundance of often conflicting advice from experts can be confusing.

When you bought this book, how many books were there beside it, giving you "expert" advice on making decisions? (Buying this one shows that you have *excellent* decision-making acumen.) Many books present "systems" for decision making, in eight, nine, twelve easy steps.

The problem with most such plans is that they are almost as intimidating as the very decision you dread making. Some plans seem to require you to have a degree in psychology or sociology to understand why you decide what you do. Others assume you have extensive experience in higher mathematics to figure out a formula. (Be honest, how many of us got through algebra with any understanding?) Other systems for decision making are so elaborate that you may need to take time off from work just to set them in motion. These are not user-friendly methods, no matter how well intentioned. And if a plan intimidates instead of liberates, it's not going to help you one whit.

MAKING THE RIGHT DECISION FOR *YOU*

Sometimes the whole point of making a decision is to make it and get on with your life. Decisions are there to move your life forward, not to delay it. And decisions should not be thought of as a burden—just think of how you'd feel if, suddenly, your right to make any decisions at all about your life was taken away.

Like choosing a brand of toothpaste or deciding whether or not to wear galoshes, some decisions are made quickly, often impulsively. Other decisions— whether to marry, how to handle a family feud— take a bit more time and reflection. In cases like these, it's important to listen to your impulses but not necessarily act impulsively. Expert systems, friends' opinions, pros and cons—all have some value in the decision-making process.

Personality does, too. Some of us are guided more

by our emotional hearts, others more by our pragmatic heads. The truth is that, regardless of personality type, none of us make decisions based purely on emotion or purely on dry facts. Human beings are a mixture of both head and heart, and both should be listened to when an important decision is on the line. Trying to isolate either head or heart and give it more value in deciding things may work against us—and may invite the virus of indecisiveness to take up permanent residence in our personality.

In the greater scheme of things, there are very few truly bad decisions. There are mistakes—born of stress, too little thought, pressures from others, fear of the alternative, risk of embarrassment . . . and born of simple human nature. Nobody's perfect, remember, not even the best decision makers. A bad mood, a withdrawn or particularly ebullient personality, having too many social obligations or none at all, a bounced check or big lottery win—all contribute to our own personal decision-making process. Other mistakes may result from relying on too little information or on misinformation. On the other hand, while we want all the facts (and the correct ones, at that) before making a decision, we can sometimes wait forever before being sure of all of them. Most people don't have that much time.

While we know that life is rarely black and white, and that we will rarely be called upon to make decisions that are completely a matter of life and death, less extreme decisions can still be daunting. In the course of our lifetimes, we'll face all kinds of decisions, small and large. Many are "no-win" decisions, unpleasant to have to make—where we'd like to avoid making any choice at all. Others are "win-win" all the way, a pleasure to deal with. Some take time, others an instant. All, difficult or easy, can be friends. All can move you—somehow—forward.

LISTENING TO YOUR OWN VOICE

There is one thing all the methods and experts have forgotten in these fast-paced and often bewildering times: the best judge of what you should be doing is *you*. It is how you feel about the decisions that affect your life that is most important. To begin to trust your own instincts is the key to overcoming the decision-making dilemma. Not for nothing did Dr. Benjamin Spock begin his best-selling parents' bible, *Baby and Child Care*, with a simple but eloquent sentence: "Trust yourself. You know more than you think you do."

And you do. That is what the Easy Decisions system—presented in this book—is all about. With the system, you will finally have a proven decision-making method that, for a change, takes into account your feelings, your instincts, both your emotional and practical sides. It is a simple and streamlined method. It doesn't take all year, doesn't require you to have several advanced degrees. The Easy Decisions system doesn't use the disembodied guidelines of faceless experts, but instead helps *you* discover *your* own instincts and the factors that *you* think are important. With this system it's possible to blast through the obstacles blocking your decision, to arrive at the most considered, satisfactory, and comfortable personal result.

It is flexible. It helps you to take into account the emotional as well as the practical, the pros and cons, the opinions of others . . . even the advice of experts. Any, all, or none can be factors if you want them to. It is *your* decision, to structure any way you see fit.

The Easy Decisions system can be used for major decisions (Should I marry? Should I put my parents in a nursing home?) as well as the less serious yet still important choices we have to make (Do I buy a pet? Do I buy or lease a car?) on a regular basis. Even if you think you are good at making decisions (and you're even better than you think you are), this system can help. Some of your mistakes, for instance, might have been avoided with just a little more thought. You can avoid even the most common lapses of judgment— that ultimately result in unhappiness and dissatisfaction—with a little advance planning.

No book, of course, can guarantee that your decisions will all be perfect or you won't make mistakes. No book can achieve your goals for you or make you happy in and of itself. But this decision system can show you which alternatives will make you happier. It will get you to weigh and evaluate your considerations, taking into account circumstances old and new that are relevant to your decision making. The Easy Decisions system teaches, in sum, the simple yet crucial art of looking before you leap, then not being afraid to leap; helping you to discover your goals and then guiding you to making rational choices that will achieve them. It will give you a precise record of how and why you reached your decision, which can help you grow and learn from the decisions you make.

And the best part is that it is you, and you alone, who will make that happen.

HOW THE EASY DECISIONS SYSTEM WORKS

We live in an age of information, but how much of the information that we have at our fingertips do we really apply to ourselves? If we are wise and true to ourselves, we can to some degree alter the courses we set for our lives. This is the guiding principle behind the Easy Decisions system, which, for the first time, brings a scientific approach to the decision-making process.

The Easy Decisions system provides a true look-before-you-leap method for deciding things, big or small. It's the best friend the undecided can have, for it's user-friendly. With this system, it's possible to *quantify* a decision and go ahead with confidence, knowing that decision was made on the basis of what *you* think is important.

With the Easy Decisions system, you'll be able to:

- Make a major decision in as little as one hour
- See—at a glance—factors and guidelines that

can influence just about any decision you can
make.

- Quantify the importance of all these factors.
- Chart your personal changes through the
  years to see how your life has changed and in
  what direction it is headed.

The Easy Decisions system is not a Yuppie I-Ching
or an astrological chart. Nor is it a complicated formula that takes an engineer's degree to decipher.
The system in itself won't necessarily make you
rich, happy, famous, or loved. It doesn't offer thin
thighs or stock-market tips and won't make you a
one-minute manager. But it will guide you to rational choices, to discover your goals and then achieve
them.

The system is a simple one, and was born from a
very real situation that happened to a friend of mine.
Frank called me one afternoon, excited over a new
job opportunity. It was a very important career decision for him. He owned his own independent con-
sulting business, but had just been offered an
important job with a large company. He liked being
independent but the thought of a large firm and a
steady, large paycheck was appealing, too.

Should he stay free-lance, or go with the new opportunity? Frank was particularly frustrated, because the traditional ways of making a decision hadn't worked for him. He had first tried listing pros and cons on a sheet of paper, and what he got was . . . a list of equal pros and equal cons. It looked something like this:

● TAKING A JOB WITH THE COMPANY ●

PROS	CONS
Steady Paycheck	Fewer Tax Deductions
More Visibility	Less Freedom
Big Office	Longer Commute
Larger Company	Won't Be Own Boss

Looking at this list, Frank saw that each option had good and bad things going for it . . . and that, upon reviewing it, he was no closer to a decision than he had been at the beginning.

So he decided to ask the opinions of others. But this backfired, too; each person he talked to had an opinion colored by what he or she wanted to do, not what Frank wanted to do. "Go into a corporate structure," said one friend. But she was having a difficult time making ends meet in her own free-lance decorating business, and was therefore negatively disposed toward being self-employed. "Keep on being your own boss," said another friend, who worked for a large company. The problem was that he was thinking of going into business for himself, and looked to Frank as a role model for doing so.

After listening to them, Frank was more confused than ever. So he decided to listen to the advice of experts. There was no shortage of books on starting your own business or succeeding in a corporate structure, but there were none to tell him what he should consider in making the leap from entrepreneur to corporation. At least none that would tell him what he didn't already know. Books on careers were too general for Frank's needs. There was simply too much advice for him to process.

"There are so many angles to consider," he sighed. Then a light bulb went on over both our heads and we decided to do just that—consider all the factors that could possibly be involved in his decision. For each factor—salary, working conditions, being his own boss vs. working for someone else—we assigned a numerical value from 1 to 10 under each option, comparing his present job vs. the new job. The number for each indicated his estimate of the relative desirability of the outcome with each option. After entering values for each of the factors, we merely added up the results. When we looked at the totals under each option, we realized something was wrong. Each factor was being treated with equal importance, so the totals were misleading. Obviously, some factors must be more important than others. So we went back over each factor and placed a weight, again from 1 to 10, that indicated how important he regarded each factor. Then we multiplied the comparative values assigned to each factor—one for each option—by the weight now attached to the factor. That did it. By adding the two columns this time, the number totals showed he really wanted to take the new job.

Our sample tally sheet looked like this:

Factor ... Weight (W)	Take Job		Stay Put	
	Value (V)	W × V	Value (V)	W × V
Freedom ... 8	5	40	10	80
Visibility ... 9	10	90	6	54
Commute ... 5	5	25	5	25
Salary ... 10	10	100	8	80
Big Office ... 5	10	50	5	25
Totals		**305**		**264**

But two days later, when he went for the final interview at the company, he discovered that the salary was not as high as originally promised. "Salary" had been one factor that was extremely important in his decision. So he went home and went back to the system we had just devised, figuring in the new information.

Frank's total in the "Take Job" option column went from 305 to 215, because he changed the "Salary" score for taking the new job from 100 to 10 (10, the weight of his factor's importance—times 1, the new value for his anticipated salary).

It turned out that the salary question was important enough to tilt his decision in the other direction, and he continued his very successful free-lance career. He was convinced he had made the right decision.

Since that time, I've used the system many times. It's helped me to decide where to spend my summer vacation, has helped my husband and me to decide if the time was right to buy a house and, once that decision was made, what town we'd live in. One couple we know used it to discover if they wanted to have a second baby; the daughter of another friend used the system to choose between two colleges. In

HARD CHOICES, EASY DECISIONS

short, the system has been used by different people for different situations. And it works.

No decision-making system is infallible, but the Easy Decisions system will keep you thinking, weighing all your options in a very tangible way. It is an open-ended method that allows for the introduction of many considerations—both practical and emotional—as you proceed with a decision. And it is a method that can be used over and over, for decisions large and small, a good tool to evaluate and re-evaluate your priorities over time.

There are a couple of additional aspects to consider. I've found that it is wise to go through the process several times over a period of time. For a variety of reasons, our best estimates of how our different factors will be affected by each of our options can vary according to our moods or new information, as can the importance we attach to each factor. Repeat the Easy Decisions system without looking at what you did earlier, then compare the results and the way you got there.

Often some of your decisions will involve or affect other people. You may want to have them participate in the process with you. My friend Frank, for example, was not married when he was offered the new job. But if he had been, his wife could have been there with him suggesting additional factors or debating with him the weights he was assigning to each of them. Or they could have gone through the process separately, and then could have compared how their individual decisions were made. By doing this, they could have better understood one another's needs and desires. (It could also have been an insurance policy for the future: if things hadn't quite worked out as planned, sharing individual and collective decisions in advance would have decreased the possibilities for later recriminations.)

The Easy Decisions system is simple to use, applicable to a wide variety of circumstances, and flexible enough to be adaptable to individual needs. The best way to understand it is to do it. And here is a sample decision, which will show you, step by step, exactly how the Easy Decisions system works.

A SAMPLE EASY DECISION —STEP BY STEP

Meet Bill Arnold. He is forty, happily married with three kids, and working as a senior vice president of a Pittsburgh advertising agency. His wife Alice is originally from Pittsburgh; Bill moved there twenty years ago from Des Moines to attend college, met and married Alice, and stayed. But Bill feels it may be time for a change. He's thinking of relocating to San Francisco because, while his job is going well in Pittsburgh, the business opportunities and fabled lifestyle in California seem both lucrative and appealing.

Unlike Frank's decision, Bill's involves more than a career move. While a better job is the basis for his decision, the change would also affect his family. A move to California would be more than a career decision; it would change not only his lifestyle, but that of his wife and children.

The thought of a move holds several drawbacks

for Bill, whose kids—ages sixteen, eleven, and eight—are happy in school where they are. Especially Tommy, the youngest, whose grades have improved since he began working with a new teacher. Bill's wife has many close friends in their neighborhood and is enjoying a new, part-time job with a local charitable organization, which is opening some potential career opportunities (in the area of corporate fund-raising) for her.

California would mean a more enjoyable lifestyle: ever since Bill took the family on vacation to Hawaii last year, the kids have been saying how much they wished they lived near the ocean, which in San Francisco is only a few minutes away. Bill's also looking at the future, thinking about how nice it would be to retire in California. He knows Alice may resist leaving the friends she has made, but he also knows that she is better at making new friends than she admits.

Bill must take into consideration divisions of opinion within the family; the children may endorse the move for reasons that aren't necessarily good for them. Some in his family may feel they are being imposed upon unfairly; sixteen-year-old Lisa may decide the boyfriend she broke up with last week is now the most important thing in her life. And Alice may resent being uprooted just as she is starting to put together business contacts and a career. Bill's decision is fraught with complexity and contradictions—clearly, merely listing pros and cons would be of little value with so many things to consider. To list pros and cons wouldn't help because it treats the factors as if they were of equal importance when obviously, in a decision of this magnitude, some factors will be much more important than others.

Using the Easy Decisions process on the other hand, will allow Bill—and Alice, who should go through the system independently—to make such an important decision based on all possible considerations, examined in relation to one another.

It's time to look at how they'll decide which option is the best for them. To begin, Bill takes a quiet afternoon to examine the possibilities. Away from distractions—in his study, over coffee at a quiet cafe, wherever he can think—Bill makes a list of considerations and factors that are important to him and to his family. With a pen and legal pad (or with a sample worksheet like those in the back of this book), Bill jots down thoughts as they come to him, in no particular order. Nothing, absolutely nothing, is too trivial to list if it means something to Bill. He can list as many factors as he wants, naming them whatever he wants. It is not necessary to put them in order of importance; what is necessary is just to put them down.

Bill begins by thinking about long-term happiness and prosperity. That's important to him, so he calls this "Good Life" and writes it down. He and Alice want to send all their children to college, so he writes down "Children's Education." He then thinks of peace of mind, which he equates with "Job Security" on the list. While his job in Pittsburgh is secure, he knows that the advertising industry is going through a shakeup and there's no indication it will quickly pull out of its current slump. Bill also knows that salaries on the West Coast might not be as handsome as they are in the East, so he lists "Salary Prospects."

He thinks of his family, and lists factors about his relatives, friends, and children's reactions to the change. His family is close to his wife's brother and sister and their two children who live nearby, but Bill thinks these family bonds may mean a bit less as his children get older and choose their friends outside the family. He lists some of these factors as "Possible Negatives on Children," "Family Closeness (Relatives)," "Effect on Social Life." Then Bill thinks of even more factors: "What if he wants to go into business for himself ("Possible Future Independence")? How much would a house cost? What about his favorite football team (Bill is a season-ticket holder)?

After about an hour, with his factors in no particular order, Bill's list of considerations looks like this:

Good Life
Salary Prospects
Job Security
Effect on Social Life
Children's Education
Possible Negatives on Children
Family Closeness (Relatives)
Amenities and Environment
Housing Costs
Retirement
Nature of Work
Job Satisfaction
Possible Future Independence
Steelers

Bill looks at this list, then decides to assign a numerical weight, on the scale from 1 to 10 (10 being most important) to each factor. As he does this—at any time in the process, in fact—he is free to add additional factors as he thinks of them, and to take away others he decides don't apply.

In assigning these numerical weights to each factor, Bill will sometimes be deciding with his heart and sometimes with his head, for some factors are more emotional and other factors more practical.

This involves some thought on Bill's part, and sometimes his answers surprise him.

Take "Job Security." How important is it for Bill? Yes, he has a family to support and a good job now, but Bill assigns this factor only a 5 in importance. Why? Because, now that he really thinks about it, he is confident that if his firm went out of business or if he were fired or if his firm merged with another, he would always be able to find another good job. He has more confidence in himself than he had thought.

Getting to the factors in random order (it's not necessary to start with the first one and work your way down), Bill looks at "Effect on Social Life." He admits to himself that, between work and raising three children, he hasn't had much of a social life. Sure, they go out with friends occasionally and entertain occasionally, but social life has not been a large, motivating factor in his and Alice's life. He also knows that both he and Alice (and the kids, too) have little trouble making and keeping friends. Bill gives "Effect on Social Life" a low weight of 3.

It takes him no time at all to assign a very high priority, a 9, to "Children's Education." Bill's parents could never afford to send him to the best schools, something Bill feels cost him in terms of advancement as an adult. He assigns "Possible Negatives on Children" only a 4 because he knows that kids are adaptable and that getting them into decent schools eventually far outweighs the possible disruption of their routines. He wants only the best for his children; education is a high priority.

Notice that all along, Bill does not compare one factor to another but instead assigns it a weight on its own, independently. And also notice that Bill doesn't agonize over whether he's assigning an emotional or a practical weight to each factor—he simply gives each the number he feels comfortable with. In some instances, he might be a bit more emotional (such as his feelings about being deprived in his scoring for "Children's Education"), in others a bit more practical (regardless of his affection for the Steelers, he gives the football team only a low factor of 2, because San Francisco, after all, does have the 49ers).

Bill assigns a high 9 to the "Good Life" factor: for him, the good life means the quality of life—climate, housing, social ties, entertainment, physical and emotional comforts for him and his family. The quality of that life is very, very important to him. "Amenities and Environment" rates a 6, because, for Bill, to live in a place with creature comforts and culture is desirable but not an absolute end in itself. "Possible Future Independence" rates a 5. Bill has been thinking that one option would be to form his own business some day; half the time he thinks it's a good idea, half the time he's content to stay with someone else's firm. He gives "Housing Costs" a 7, which is a high rating; it's important that he and his family have a decent place to live, the best possible within the limits of Bill and Alice's income.

Bill continues to examine each factor and see how each one rates in importance. When he is through with his soul-searching, Bill's list looks like this:

Good Life ... 9
Salary Prospects ... 8
Job Security ... 5
Children's Education ... 9
Possible Negatives on Children ... 4
Family Closeness (Relatives) ... 3
Amenities and Environment ... 6
Housing Costs ... 7
Retirement ... 5
Nature of Work ... 6
Job Satisfaction ... 6
Possible Future Independence ... 5
Steelers ... 2

Having weighed each factor on his list, Bill now writes two headings (options) at the top of the page, to the right of the factors. First, he writes: "To Move." Next to that, he writes the other heading: "Stay Put."

Now it's time for Bill to estimate the probable outcome for each factor on his list as a result of each of his two choices—considering how each factor would be affected by either moving or by staying in Pittsburgh. The first factor is "Good Life." Bill must assign a 1 to 10 value for both Pittsburgh and San Francisco. Ten, as usual, is the most desirable—the best possible outcome relating to that factor.

Bill's life isn't miserable now. In fact, it's comfortable. He is not poor, his children are healthy and happy, his wife involved. Still, he feels something is lacking—opportunity, maybe. He feels he's not operating to capacity, and that he could make more money and provide a better life in California. When he considers his future in the East, his thoughts just don't sparkle as he wishes they would. For the "Good Life" factor, Bill gives the "To Move" column a rating of 8, and the "Stay Put" column gets a rating of 6.

He then takes the "Amenities and Environment" factor. Bill considers Pittsburgh, the "Stay Put" column. It's an older city, and the area is too built up and industrial for Bill's taste. His life there is comfortable, but everything feels a bit worn. Good private schools are expensive, and the climate is harsh, especially in winter. Fresh vegetables are expensive and hard to find in the off-season, and to get to the beach involves a major excursion. Bill gives the "Stay Put" column a rating of 5. Next, he considers San Francisco's environment and amenities. The mild climate, beautiful scenery, good public school system,year-round abundance of fresh food (not to mention a cornucopia of restaurants), and the feeling of more physical space all add up for Bill: he gives "To Move" a value of 9.

On the football front, Bill knows that San Francisco has a great team, so he wouldn't be deprived of his favorite pastime. He rates "to Move" a 3 in this category. But he has always been a devoted and loyal Steelers fan. He really loves that team. Bill gives the "Stay Put" column a 7 for this factor. Under "Family Closeness (Relatives)," Bill knows that if they move he and Alice and the kids will meet new friends, but family is important to them. Knowing that their blood relatives are nearby is a comforting thought to his family; they not only get along, but they are close. Bill puts an 8 in the "Stay Put" column for family closeness; a 1 in the "To Move" column (neither Bill nor Alice has relatives or close friends in San Francisco).

Factor by factor, Bill goes through his list in relation to the options "To Move" or "Stay Put," assigning relative values. Bill knows that real estate is cheaper in the East and that San Francisco is very desirable (hence, more expensive). Under "Housing Costs," he rates "To Move" a 5 and "Stay Put" a 7. The San Francisco area has several prestigious universities that Bill knows would be wonderful for his kids to attend; Pittsburgh has good colleges and universities, too, but Bill believes that the stature and variety of curriculum in San Francisco is better. So for "Children's Education," he gives "To Move" an 8 value and "Stay Put" a value of 5. Looking to his own future, Bill thinks of "Retirement." How does he see himself when he's in his sixties? Does he want to spend his retirement in Pittsburgh, with its cold winters, or San Francisco, where the weather is more temperate and sunny? If he has more leisure time on his hands, which locale has the greater variety of activities to choose from? For this factor, Bill rates "To Move" an 8, "Stay Put" a 6.

Bill continues this way down his list, going through each factor in relation to moving or staying put. When he is finished, his list looks like this:

	To Move	Stay Put
Good Life ... 9	8	6
Salary Prospects ... 8	8	5
Job Security ... 3	6	7
Effect on Social Life ... 3	5	7
Children's Education ... 9	8	5
Possible Negatives on Children ... 4	5	7
Family Closeness (Relatives) ... 3	1	8
Amenities and Environment ... 6	9	5
Housing Costs ... 7	5	7
Retirement ... 5	8	6
Nature of Work ... 6	7	5
Job Satisfaction ... 6	8	5
Possible Future Independence ... 5	7	5
Steelers ... 2	3	7

This done, Bill is ready for the next stage, and it's an easy one. He will multiply the original weight assigned to each factor by the value he has assigned to each option column ("To Move," "Stay Put"). For example, in "Family Closeness," he multiplies the factor's weight of 3 by the "To Move" value of 1. The number Bill gets in this case is 3, and he places it to the right of the original number in the "To Move" column.

Then Bill moves to the "Stay Put" column and multiplies 3 (weight) by his "Stay Put" value of 8, giving him the sum of 24, which he places to the right in the "Stay Put" column.

When Bill has multiplied all the factors' weights and values, he then adds up the two columns of multiplied numbers. His finished chart looks like this:

Factor ... Weight (W)	To Move		Stay Put	
	Value (V)	W × V	Value (V)	W × V
Good Life ... 9	8	72	6	54
Salary Prospects ... 8	8	64	5	40
Job Security ... 5	6	30	7	35
Effect on Social Life ... 3	5	15	7	21
Children's Education ... 9	8	72	5	45
Possible Negatives on Children ... 4	5	20	7	28
Family Closeness (Relatives) ... 3	1	3	8	24
Amenities and Environment ... 6	9	54	5	30
Housing Costs ... 7	5	35	7	49
Retirement ... 5	8	40	6	30
Nature of Work ... 6	7	42	5	30
Job Satisfaction ... 6	8	48	5	30
Possible Future Independence ... 5	7	35	5	25
Steelers ...2	3	6	7	14
Totals		**536**		**455**

With a score of 536 ("To Move") and 455 ("Stay Put"), Bill concludes that his right decision would be to move. He might even be surprised that his decision is not nearly as close a call as he originally thought.

Of course, Bill can run through the system again whenever he wants. He may reassess his factors and the weights he has given them at any point. He might add new factors or eliminate others as well. Perhaps this time around, in the cafe, he was a bit distracted. Perhaps later he'll think of other factors ("Physical Activity," "Creative Activity," "Cultural Proximity," "Stress," to name a few) that he didn't put in before. Perhaps he'd like to take one of his initial factors—"Good Life"—and break it down into individual components like "Weather," "Relaxation," "Fun Activities" to further sharpen how the system reflects what he wants. No factor is too trivial to include if he feels that it is relevant to his decision.

With the Easy Decisions system, Bill is free to let his mind bring up anything, no matter how remotely connected it is to the issue before him. And he is free to run through the system as many times as he likes. In some cases, like deciding on where to vacation, once might be enough. But for Bill, whose decision is a complicated one and involves not only himself but his family, it might be comforting to run through it again. Just as there are many factors that affect his decision, so too are there many factors that can interfere with his thought process in making the decision. Maybe Bill has had a particularly bad day or is in a bad mood. Maybe he's tired, or has come from a particularly enjoyable gathering with his relatives.

It's a given that your age, moods, pressure from others, stress at work, cycles of the moon, the current state of your health or your bank book, a particularly depressing or uplifting movie—any and all of these outside factors can influence how you feel and what factors are important to you. Outside pressures can make you feel elated or gloomy, and all can have an impact on your capacity to make a decision.

In such a decision, Bill won't be the only one doing the system. Alice, too, will take some time to decide what factors are important to her, and give those factors her own ratings. Alice should do this independently, and when she's through, she'll sit down with Bill and they'll compare what each of them thinks is important and what each of them decided via the Easy Decisions system. (Here the system provides an extra bonus of being an effective tool of communication as well as a decision-making mechanism.) At some juncture, Alice and Bill could do a chart together, to get a shared sense of what the considerations are for each and both of them.

By using the system individually and together, Bill and Alice have increased their chances for a mutually satisfying final decision. Their choice will be the result of full participation by both of them, which lessens the chances for future recriminations by either party; everything is out in the open beforehand. And, by making a decision using this method, Bill and Alice's horizons have been considerably widened: it's likely that Alice has thought of some factors Bill hasn't, and vice versa.

• MAKING *YOUR* DECISIONS •

Giving the factors you've chosen a number is not an arbitrary decision, of course. But at the same time it's important to trust your own instincts in assigning weights. Remember, this is *your* decision and no one else's. If you were in the same situation as Bill, you might have some factors in mind you think he should have considered, and you might discard some he thought important. And you might have weighed some of his factors differently: if you loved football more than Bill, for instance, and wanted to give "Steelers" a 10, that's your prerogative. The Easy Decisions system works because it is a system built on what's right for you, not what other people think is right for you. Structure it any way you want.

However you do structure it, keep a copy to refer to later, for the system can also chart how your life changes. Lives and the important factors in those lives do change, of course—by design and by themselves. Obviously, if Bill were considering a move when he was in his twenties with no children, some of the factors important to him might be very different from what they are now that he's a man of forty. And if Bill were deciding at age sixty whether or not to move, with his children grown, his factors and the weights he assigns to them might be different still. How intriguing for both him and Alice to look at their work sheets down the road and see what changed and what stayed the same!

Life, of course, is a complex maze of change and growth. Sometimes we move forward by design, sometimes external factors push us along. Sometimes it's not easy, but by using the Easy Decisions system, these transitions can be made more understandable. And this is the strong point of the Easy Decisions system. More than just a way of making an immediate decision, our system can be a "life planner," as well. By saving the worksheets from a particular decision and reviewing them from time to time, you can see what factors in your life have been important to you, what factors still are, and what you've outgrown. Easy Decisions can also be used as a chart for change ... and growth: a concise, thoughtful, and nonbulky scrapbook of your interests and feelings and thoughts throughout the years.

• USING THIS BOOK •

As you will see in the following examples, different decisions call for different kinds of factors and considerations. The factors listed in this book's case studies and worksheets are there simply as guidelines and not as rules to follow. Feel free to use, discard, or add to them, for they are here simply to show how Easy Decisions can work in a variety of situations.

Next, you'll see the kinds of decisions—large, medium, and small, if you will—that the system can help you make. You'll see a series of very different case studies and get a glimpse of how others have used the system to make decision making a constructive and enlightening process . . . instead of a nerve-wracking one.

The Easy Decisions system *is* easy. And friendly. It provides both a practical decision-making tool and a valuable record of some of the most important— and most exciting—moments of your life. Now let's get started.

THE EASY DECISIONS SYSTEM AT WORK

In the sections that follow we will describe case studies that can show you how other people have used this system to make decisions. We'll look at a broad range of different kinds of decisions—from simple to complicated, from mundane to dramatic. Easy Decisions will work for all these cases—whenever there is a choice between at least two alternatives. And keep this in mind: deciding whether to do something or to do nothing *is* a choice with consequences either way.

Decisions involving three or more options can be even more bewildering. The system can be particularly useful in these situations because it forces you to focus on one factor at a time—for any number of options. You'll be surprised at how simple the most complicated decisions can be as Easy Decisions helps you sort out what is important to you. Also, getting it all down on paper will make it easier to keep everything in perspective.

It's time to examine some real-life case studies. But remember, the examples that follow are based on what other people have considered relevant to their personal decisions. Their case histories are presented only as examples, which you can tailor to your own needs and values, to make your own easy decisions.

• EDUCATION CHOICES •

In this case study we'll see the kind of decision that many families and students face when contemplating the next step in their education. While it involves a college student, the steps involved could also be used to decide whether to attend college at all, whether to go back to college, or, for adults, whether to get another degree or attend night school. No matter what the case, it shows how to define your individual goals to help you reach an important decision.

Nancy is a seventeen-year-old girl who grew up and still lives in Maplewood, New Jersey, a middle-class suburban community about ten miles outside of Newark. She is the oldest of three children; her father is an accountant, and her mother works part time at a gift shop. Nancy has been a good student, but not a great one, and she, like many of her girl-friends, is facing a decision about college.

Nancy has been happy in high school. She is a

cheerleader, has plenty of friends, hasn't exactly hated studying—but she hasn't exactly loved it either. And as she put it, "I don't have a clue about what I want to do when I grow up." When she tries to think about college or a career or even "The Future," her mind races around from thought to thought until she winds up in her room watching television, eating microwaved popcorn.

Nancy is in her senior year in school and starting to feel desperate. Her guidance counselor at school gave her advice: "Well, dear, decide what you want to do." Nancy almost laughed in the woman's face, because that was precisely what Nancy was hoping the guidance counselor would tell her. But Nancy was smart enough to know that no one could tell her what she really wanted for herself.

In a way, Nancy's decision was more complicated than some kids' her age because her parents, though not wealthy, had put aside money every year for her college education, so financial considerations did not limit her choices. In this case, as well as in a variety of others, having enough money to do things has created its own problems by opening up the number of choices available.

Nancy needed tools to help her figure out for herself what was truly important to her, to find a way to clarify and organize her scattered thoughts and feelings.

In Nancy's case it was useful to work through the Easy Decisions system for two different decisions involving college. The first issue was whether she wanted to go to college at all. Nancy's mother and father were very eager for Nancy to go to college, but knew that that should not be the only reason for her to go. Nancy was, in fact, trying not to do the opposite of what her parents wanted simply as a reaction to their wishes.

The first step in the process was to determine what the first set of choices was. Obviously, one choice was "To Go to College." The other option could have been "Not to Go to College." But Nancy needed to make the alternative more specific than not going to college because it would then be easier to imagine the consequences of that choice. Nancy came up with "Get a Job." With her alternatives decided, Nancy got a pad and a pencil and began making a list of the factors that might be involved in her decision. Her mother helped by asking Nancy if this or that was a factor she might want to consider, but she was very good about urging her daughter to put down only what Nancy thought was a factor for herself, and not to include something because she thought it might please her mother.

Nancy wrote "Living Away from Home" as her first factor. After the first entry the others came quickly:

Living Away from Home
Social Life
Being a Cheerleader
Learning
Studying
Learning about Life
Meeting New Friends
Being in Touch with Old Friends
Getting a College Degree
Career Opportunities
Meeting Mr. Right
Traveling
Being Away from Brothers
Being Away from Parents

After going back over the list to assign a weight to each factor reflecting the importance each held for her, Nancy's entries looked like this:

Living Away from Home ... 4
Social Life ... 9
Being a Cheerleader ... 3
Learning ... 3

Studying ... −7
Learning about Life ... 5
Meeting New Friends ... 7
Being in Touch with Old Friends ... 9
Getting a College Degree ... 6
Career Opportunities ... 7
Meeting Mr. Right ... 4
Traveling ... 8
Being Away from Brothers ... −2
Being Away from Parents ... −3

Note that three factors—studying, being away from her brothers, and being away from her parents—have negative weights. Negative weights are as important to consider and include in the Easy Decisions system as positive ones. (Note that negative numbers work the same way as positive ones: a negative 1 weight indicates a relatively unimportant, but negative factor; a negative 10 indicates a very important negative factor.) They should play as much a role as positive factors in reaching a decision if they are of any importance to you. What was of particular interest to Nancy was that at first she had entered positive numbers for being away from her brothers, but after a little imagining of what it would be like for the first time not to have those "mean, little pests" around, she realized, to her surprise, that she would really miss them ... although not that much, because she only gave the factor a negative 2.

After setting up the columns with the two choices: "Going to College" and "Getting a Job," and then fixing a number that was her best estimate of the relative value of each choice—for each factor—her chart now looked like this:

	Going to College	Getting a Job
Living Away from Home ... 4	10	0
Social Life ... 9	10	5
Being a Cheerleader... 3	4	0
Learning ... 3	5	2
Studying ... −7	4	0
Learning about Life ... 5	1	7
Meeting New Friends ... 7	8	2
Being in Touch with Old Friends ... 9	4	6
Getting a College Degree ... 6	5	0
Career Opportunities ... 7	8	2
Meeting Mr. Right ... 4	8	1
Traveling ... 8	2	7
Being Away from Brothers ... −2	8	0
Being Away from Parents ... −3	8	0

After multiplying the values for each option by the weight she attached to them, Nancy's finished chart looked like this:

Factor ... Weight (W)	Going to College		Getting a Job	
	Value (V)	W × V	Value (V)	W × V
Living Away from Home ... 4	10	40	0	0
Social Life ... 9	10	90	5	45
Being a Cheerleader ... 3	4	12	0	0
Learning ... 3	5	15	2	6
Studying ... −7	4	−28	0	0
Learning about Life ... 5	1	5	7	35
Meeting New Friends ... 7	8	56	2	14
Being in Touch with Old Friends ... 9	4	36	6	54
Getting a College Degree ... 6	5	30	0	0
Career Opportunities ... 7	8	56	2	14
Meeting Mr. Right ... 4	8	32	1	4
Traveling ... 8	2	16	7	56
Being Away from Brothers −... 2	8	−16	0	0
Being Away from Parents −... 3	8	−24	0	0
Totals		**320**		**228**

When Nancy showed her chart to her mother, her mother breathed a deep sigh of relief. She hadn't realized how much she had wanted her daughter to go to college. Now Nancy realized that college was important to her, too.

The next choice was which college to apply to. When Nancy thought of college, she considered Rutgers because most of her friends were applying there, and while it was away from home, it was only an hour away. She had once visited Skidmore in Saratoga, New York, and thought that was very pretty, and she had heard it was a good school. Her best friend's older sister was going to Boston University and said that the Boston area was filled with colleges, and the social life "has to be the best in the world."

When Nancy explained to her mother the three choices she had in mind and the information she was relying on to select those three, her mother urged her to go to the library and look at the college catalogues of those schools as well as others she might find there. She also bought a book that described most of the schools in America, and the two of them went through the book together. (Obviously, the more facts you have about how each factor will be colored by each option, the more likely that your decision will rest on a firm foundation.) When their research was completed, Nancy and her mother sat down together to begin the system again—this time to figure out which college to attend: Rutgers, Skidmore, or Boston University.

Nancy was able to use some of the same factors she had listed for her first decision:

Social Life
Being a Cheerleader
Career Opportunities
Meeting New Friends
Contact with Old Friends
Meeting Mr. Right

Then she added to the list those additional factors that seemed important to her:

Academic Reputation
Variety of Courses
Difficulty
Big School
Junior-Year-Abroad Program
Closeness to Home
Winning Football Team

When Nancy assigned numbers (weights) to each of the factors, her list looked like this:

Social Life ... 9
Being a Cheerleader ... 3
Career Opportunities ... 7

Meeting New Friends ... 7
Contact with Old Friends ... 9
Meeting Mr. Right ... 4
Academic Reputation ... 8
Variety of Courses ... 7
Difficulty ... 9
Big School ... 5
Junior-Year-Abroad Program ... 7
Closeness to Home ... 4
Winning Football Team ... 3

Nancy's step was to set up the columns with her three choices: "Rutgers," "Skidmore," and "Boston University," and then assign a number that was her best estimate of how well each factor would fare under each college choice. Her chart now looked like this:

	Rutgers	Skidmore	B.U.
Social Life ... 9	7	6	5
Being a Cheerleader ... 3	7	0	5
Career Opportunities ... 7	8	5	6
Meeting New Friends ... 7	5	7	9
Contact with Old Friends ... 9	8	2	3
Meeting Mr. Right ... 4	6	1	8
Academic Reputation ... 8	7	6	5
Variety of Courses ... 7	8	5	6
Difficulty ... 9	8	5	6
Big School ... 5	7	3	9
Junior-Year-Abroad Program ... 7	2	8	6
Closeness to Home ... 4	9	6	5
Winning Football Team ... 3	9	0	9

After multiplying the values for each option by the weight she had attached to the respective factors, Nancy's finished chart for colleges looked like this:

	Rutgers		Skidmore		B.U.	
Social Life ... 9	7	63	6	54	5	45
Being a Cheerleader ... 3	7	21	0	0	5	15
Career Opportunities ... 7	8	56	5	35	6	42
Meeting New Friends ... 7	5	35	7	49	9	63
Contact with Old Friends ... 9	8	72	2	18	3	27
Meeting Mr. Right ... 4	6	24	1	4	8	32
Academic Reputation ... 8	7	56	6	48	5	40
Variety of Courses ... 7	8	56	5	35	6	42
Difficulty ... 9	8	72	5	45	6	54
Big School ... 5	7	35	3	15	9	45
Junior-Year-Abroad Program ... 7	2	14	8	56	6	42
Closeness to Home ... 4	9	36	6	24	5	20
Winning Football team ... 3	9	27	0	0	9	27
Totals		**567**		**383**		**494**

The decision was there for Nancy, as well as her mother, to see. Easy Decisions helped Nancy to decide—first, that she really did want to go to college, and, second, that Rutgers was her first choice. On re-examining the list and the values she attached to the factors, the reasons why she made the choices she did were even clearer to Nancy. Her social life at college was an important component that made a big difference in how she valued her options. Career opportunities were also important to her, but each of her choices would provide opportunities and the discrepancies were not that large. Boston University was greatly favored over Rutgers for the likelihood of meeting new friends, but the difference was more than offset by the ability of Nancy to stay in contact with her old friends if she attended Rutgers. Most of the other factors were quite close but usually favored Rutgers. Skidmore, looking back at it, was clearly never a contender, but until going through the system, Nancy hadn't realized that.

She felt comfortable with her choice, but she will probably go through Easy Decisions again before making a final decision, just to double-check.

Nancy might find that, once her decision is made, the Easy Decisions system will come in handy in the future when making other decisions—such as deciding what major to choose, whether or not to join a sorority or get involved in extracurricular activities, whether to stay at her chosen college or to transfer to another one, and, eventually, whether or not to go on to graduate school.

RELATIONSHIP DECISIONS

Sometimes when we have to deal with decisions that have powerful emotional aspects, we can become paralyzed. These kinds of decisions often involve conflicts between what seem like equally strong pulls leading us in opposite directions. The Easy Decisions system can be very helpful in such situations because it forces you to focus on the pulls and be as objective as you can in determining just how important each factor is. In confronting emotional decisions it is especially important to repeat the system several times over a period of time to learn how constant your feelings are.

While the example that follows concerns divorce, the Easy Decisions system can also be useful in making other relationship decisions: whether to get married at all, whether to live with someone, if and when to break off a relationship that is going badly, whether or not to become more deeply involved in a romantic relationship in the first place. The system comes in handy in evaluating friendships, too: personal growth and change effect our nonromantic relationships with men and women friends and family members, as well.

Julie is thirty-four years old and has been married to Mark for eight years. They live in a co-op in New York City with their five-year-old daughter, Molly. Within a year after Julie gave birth, she became convinced that the marriage was terminal. She and Mark rarely speak, at least about things that are important. And their sexual relationship has been virtually nonexistent since the time of her pregnancy. She has suggested to Mark that they see a marriage counselor, but he is adamantly opposed to the idea. He insists that they are doing fine.

Before their marriage and until Molly was born, Julie was an editor at a woman's magazine. Mark is a stockbroker who has been earning close to $100,000 a year. Julie has been wanting to go back to work now that Molly has started school, but this has led to arguments with Mark, who wants her to stay home. To add to Julie's quandary, Mark recently discovered that he has diabetes. He is taking insulin on a daily basis.

Julie's parents got a divorce when she was a teenager and she remembers only too well how devastating that was to her. She is also frightened about the prospect of being alone in the single world. What with AIDS, and the seemingly depleted supply of available men around, she imagines herself being even more lonely than she is now. She also feels that if she left Mark now that he is sick, she would feel terrible guilt for abandoning her husband. After all, she had promised to be with him through sickness as well as health.

On the other hand, Julie is convinced that Molly is suffering by the clear lack of affection between her parents. Mark says he loves Molly but he hardly spends any time with her. Julie has tried to be a "perfect" wife, but she feels if she continues on in the same way for very much longer, she'll have a nervous breakdown. And that would be a disaster for Molly.

Two years ago Julie began seeing a psychologist twice a week. Her sessions have helped her get in touch with her anger about the way Mark has treated her, but it hasn't helped her make a decision about what she should do about her marriage. The therapist has urged her not to make any major decisions until she feels she better understands herself. This seemed like sensible advice when she first heard it, but now she's starting to think she may spend the rest of her life trying to better understand herself, and by the time she may feel confident about her "psycho-history," her life could be well on its way to being over.

A week ago Julie found Mark's diary, and against her better judgment (but without much guilt) she went through it. She found a number of entries where Mark was having meetings, drinks, and dinners with a woman called Tammy. Julie was surprised to realize that she didn't much care that Mark was having an affair. She resolved to make a decision and make it soon, one way or the other. She couldn't put her life on hold, nor could she wait forever.

Julie decided to use the Easy Decisions system to decide what to do. She saw her choices as "Divorce" and "Remain with Mark," and wrote them on top of a piece of paper. Then she began her list of factors:

> Living without Mark
> Living Alone
> Not Cooking for Mark
> Abandoning Mark
> Effect on Molly
> Setting Up a New House
> Financial Burden
> Working Again
> Dating
> Finding a New Husband
> Being Independent

Attitude of Friends
Losing Friends
Making New Friends
Disappointment of Parents
Traveling

After going back over the list to assign a weight for each factor reflecting the importance each held for her, Julie's entries looked like this:

Living without Mark ... 8
Living Alone ... −5
Not Cooking for Mark ... 4
Abandoning Mark ... 3
Effect on Molly ... 10
Setting Up a New House ... −5
Financial Burden ... −5
Working Again ... 9
Dating ... −4
Finding a New Husband ... −4
Being Independent ... 9
Attitude of Friends ... 3
Losing Friends ... 3
Making New Friends ... 4
Disappointment of Parents ... 2
Traveling ... 4

Several factors such as "Setting Up a New House," "Financial Burden," and "Working Again" seem related, if not overlapping. Similarly, "Living Alone" would entail "Living without Mark" and "Not Cooking for Mark". The Easy Decisions system can accommodate these overlaps. As long as *Julie* has a clear idea of the differences between the factors and what they mean to her as she applies them to the choices, the system will work.

Easy Decisions helps you to focus on the larger considerations of your decision and to break those considerations down into their sometimes conflicting components. If you assign a weight to a factor, but on reviewing it want to change it, you should try to analyze why. It may be because you realize there are other aspects to that factor. If that is the case, those other factors should be listed separately and given a weight of their own. Once the components are isolated they can be more accurately weighed.

Julie, for example, when she began weighing her list of factors, assigned a high, positive number to "Living without Mark," but then she thought about the prospect of living alone and felt a little scared, so she properly listed "Living Alone" as a separate factor and assigned a negative number to it. Then she realized that living without Mark would also mean not cooking for him, and the idea of not cooking for him seemed of such special importance, it justified in Julie's mind the addition of that as an additional factor. On the other hand, she decided to eliminate the "Abandoning Mark" factor; if he had enough energy to have an affair, his diabetes was obviously not life-threatening.

After setting up the columns with the two choices—"Divorce" and "Remain with Mark"—and then fixing a number that was her best estimate of how each factor would be affected by each choice, Julie's chart now looked like this:

	Divorce	Remain with Mark
Living without Mark ... 8	10	0
Living Alone ... −5	8	0
Not Cooking for Mark ... 4	10	0
Effect on Molly ... 10	−5	−5
Setting Up a New House ... −5	10	0
Financial Burden ... −5	8	1
Working Again ... 9	10	0
Dating ... −4	10	0
Finding a New Husband ... −4	8	0
Being Independent ... 9	8	2
Attitude of Friends ... 3	4	2
Losing Friends ... 3	8	1
Making New Friends ... 4	8	2
Disappointment of Parents ... 2	8	0
Traveling ... 4	8	1

You see that several factors received a 0 under the choice of remaining with Mark. This is the way the Easy Decisions system accommodates a situation where something will happen if one option is chosen, but where nothing will occur if the other option is selected.

After multiplying the factors for each option by the weight she attached to them, Julie's chart looked like this:

	Divorce		Remain with Mark	
Living without Mark ... 8	10	80	0	0
Living Alone ... −5	8	−40	0	0
Not Cooking for Mark ... 4	10	40	0	0
Effect on Molly ... 10	−5	−50	−5	−50
Setting Up a New House ... −5	10	−50	0	0
Financial Burden ... −5	8	−40	1	−5
Working Again ... 9	10	90	0	0
Dating ... −4	10	−40	0	0
Finding a New Husband ... −4	8	−32	0	0
Being Independent ... 9	8	72	2	18
Attitude of Friends ... 3	4	12	2	6
Losing Friends ... 3	8	24	1	3
Making New Friends ... 4	8	32	2	8
Disappointment of Parents ... 2	8	16	0	0
Traveling ... 4	8	32	1	4
Totals		**146**		**−16**

Julie's choice of remaining with Mark has a negative total. This is not unusual for the system. Sometimes you will find that *both* choices will be negative. This reflects the fact that, at times, we have to deal with decisions where we, unfortunately, must choose between the lesser of two evils.

In cases where all the choices we have worked through turn out to be negative, we should ask ourselves if there are any other options we can consider. Is doing nothing and keeping the status quo a better option? If not, and if it's impossible to avoid making a decision, then we should choose the least negative option.

When comparing the effect of each factor, Julie was upset to realize that the effect on Molly, which Julie regarded as the most important factor, would be significantly negative with both options she was considering. Sometimes this is a reality we have to accept. In this case, however, Julie could just as easily have viewed the consequences positively, and the results of the system would have been the same. Julie assigned a negative number to divorcing Mark because she was thinking of the loss for Molly of not having her father in the house. And when Julie was thinking of remaining with Mark, she was considering the negative effect on Molly of continuing in the unhappy marriage atmosphere, where Molly frequently saw her mother crying.

After focusing on how she had handled the entries for the effect on Molly, Julie realized that she could also view the options positively. She could assign a positive number under divorce because it would be good for Molly to be out of the unhappy environment of Julie's marriage, and she could also assign a positive number to remaining with Mark because of the positive value to Molly of his presence in the house. This was like viewing the glass as either half empty or half full.

Another aspect of this most important factor was initially upsetting to Julie: the effect on Molly, whether viewed negatively or positively, was not really having an impact on Julie's decision. Since the numbers assigned to the options for that factor were the same, either a negative 5 or a positive 5, when multiplied by the weight assigned to that factor, either choice produced the same number—thereby, in a sense, canceling each other out. The Easy Decisions system was again working properly because this showed Julie that she had to think more carefully to focus on whether she had overlooked any effects on Molly.

In the end Julie was satisfied that she had taken into consideration what was most important. And Julie then knew that, ironically, while the effect on Molly was the most important factor for her, Julie's decision was actually being determined by the other factors.

Looking at the results of what her worksheet was telling her, Julie knew she had a clear choice. She felt the process was enormously informative, but she wasn't sure she could act on it immediately. If she didn't act on it, she would know there were other factors that were holding her back. Easy Decisions could also assist her in this way—it would prompt her to search her mind and heart for those other factors preventing her from making the decision that her chart indicated. Or it would force her to reconsider the values she was placing on the factors that she had thought were important.

Julie decided to wait a bit and explore other factors. She knows that divorce is probably the best thing for her to do, and she is using the system as a tool to be more sure of herself.

Whatever Julie decides to do, Easy Decisions has already provided an important future document for Julie and perhaps even for Molly when she grows up. With it, both mother and daughter will have a record of how seriously Julie had thought about her decision and the basis of that decision. It may also be a comfort for Molly to see how her mother's regard for her was central to her decision.

• FAMILY DECISIONS •

Often the decisions we must make are colored by what other people say we should do, or think we should do. Our next example deals with a very basic decision for most couples: whether or not to have a child. At the same time, the Easy Decisions system can be used for other family decisions—whether to adopt, give a home to a foster child, have a parent come to live with you, how to blend stepchildren and your own children into your marriage, how to deal with in-laws, whether to lend money to a family member . . . or ask for some. From the most basic decisions to the less-earthshaking ones (going on a joint vacation with your parents, for example), the system is here to help.

Paula and Andy decided to use the system together to make a major decision: whether or not to have a child. Andy, who is fifteen years older than Paula, was married before and his two children from that marriage have graduated from college. Paula is thirty-seven and travels a good deal in her position as a marketing representative for a large corporation. They've been married for five years and the question of having a child is a big one. Andy is enthusiastic; Paula is not so sure.

Their first step was to fill out the worksheet separately, each discovering the important factors in such a decision. Andy's chart looked like this:

	Child		No Child	
Finances ... 6	5	30	9	54
Enjoying the Child ... 7	6	42	0	0
Improve on Past ... 8	6	48	0	0
Sleepless Nights ... − 5	4	− 20	0	0
Quality of Life ... 8	5	40	6	48
Career Interruption ... − 2	5	− 10	0	0
Paula Relationship ... 8	8	64	5	40
Totals		**194**		**142**

Andy's financial commitments to the children from his first marriage are at an end, and he thinks that both his relationship with Paula and his life would be enriched by their having a child of their own. He's been through it before, and is eager to make up for some of the mistakes he made with his children first time around; he is convinced he'd be a better father.

Paula had some of Andy's considerations, plus a few of her own. Here's her list:

	Child		No Child	
Career Track ... 8	2	16	7	56
Mothering Feelings ... 4	5	20	2	8
Finances ... 5	3	15	6	30
Peace and Quiet ... 8	2	16	5	40
Time with Andy ... 7	2	14	4	28
Biological Clock ... 5	8	40	0	0
Living Space ... 5	2	10	5	25
Fear of Mistakes ... 7	6	42	2	14
Totals		**173**		**201**

Paula was able to see practical things from her list—how important her job, peace and quiet, and Andy were to her. She also discovered that her biggest fears about having a child had to do with repeating the mistakes her mother had made; she was surprised to see that her maternal instinct rated high in the "No Child" column—Paula has always enjoyed being around her friends' children, although she'd never thought much about having one of her own.

Both Paula and Andy knew that doing their separate lists was just the beginning, a way of opening up about their individual concerns, fears and hopes about starting a family. One night they decided to fill out the worksheet together to see what would happen. They began by exchanging their own lists of factors. Paula hadn't realized how important improving on the past was to Andy; Andy began to understand how important Paula's career was to her.

Paul and Andy then made a factor list together, discussing each one on the list. Some factors were mostly Andy's, others were Paula's, others were mutual concerns. They both talked about how a child might affect their life together, their vacations, their careers, even their sex lives. Their factor list, with weights mutually decided upon, looked like this:

Paula's Career ... 8
Andy Time with Child ... 8
Vacation Travel ... 5
Living Space ... 5
Family Closeness ... 8
Sex ... 5
Time Alone ... 5

Housework ... 4
Social Life ... 4
Andy as Dad ... 8

This next step was to assign values to the Child/ No Child options for each factor:

	Child		No Child	
Paula's Career ... 8	5	40	9	72
Andy Time with Child ... 8	6	48	0	0
Vacation Travel ... 5	5	25	9	45
Living Space ... 5	3	15	5	25
Family Closeness ... 8	8	64	5	40
Sex ... 5	5	25	7	35
Time Alone ... 5	4	20	8	40
Housework ... 4	2	8	5	20
Social Life ... 4	4	16	5	20
Andy as Dad ... 8	9	72	0	0
Totals		**333**		**297**

Both Paula and Andy were happily surprised by what they discovered: that family closeness would benefit, that time spent with their child was an important factor and doable, that the obstacles they had thought about—vacation travel, social life, and living space—could be worked out if they had a baby. Certainly there would be adjustments that would have to be made, but working through the Easy De-cisions system together reassured Paula that Andy didn't expect her to give up her work, and would spend lots of time with the baby. Andy was happy to know that Paula was not as dead set against a baby as he had thought—it was almost as if, by putting her fears down on paper, she had conquered some of them.

By using the system to define their fears and hopes together, Paula and Andy opened up a line of com-munication that had been missing in their marriage. In this case, working through the Easy Decisions system together was an important first step in de-ciding to start a family. There was a lot to talk about now that they knew what concrete factors were im-portant to each and to both.

The dialogue was just beginning. Paula and Andy began to think of other factors—how much time each was willing to give to the baby so that the other could have a break, what dreams they had for the child who might share their lives, how a baby might change their day-to-day lives in positive and nega-tive ways, where in the house the crib would go, if they should hire professional child care, whether they should get a puppy, how much maternity leave

Paula's company would give her. No factor was too trivial to put down, especially in this most crucial of decisions.

Paula and Andy felt they weren't quite ready to have a child immediately, but by using the system they discovered that they both truly wanted to try in the future. This decision alone was a big one. They decided to wait a couple of months and do some individual thinking about the consequences of having a child, then scheduled a night where they would sit down and do the system together again to see how their thoughts had jelled. Throughout their decision-making process, Paula and Andy used our system, not just as a tool to quantify a final decision, but as a barometer to measure their feelings and growth—individually and as a couple.

• MULTIPLE CHOICES •

There aren't always just two options to consider when making a decision, of course. In the case of Nancy's deciding on the college of her choice, her decision was a part of a larger decision—whether to go to college at all. Few choices are clearly either/or; often there are many possible options to choose from, each with its own set of values to consider for the list of factors.

Next, we'll consider an example in which several choices were available: deciding if and where to buy a house.

Deciding where to live is an emotional issue, as well as a practical one, and, given the economy these days, an increasingly complicated one. Shelter—the place we call home—is a necessity, and involves one of the most important decisions we'll ever make.

Judi and David, a New York couple in their late thirties with two small children, used Easy Decisions to decide where they would buy their first house. Their two-bedroom apartment was obviously too small, and they had saved enough for a down payment—David is a lawyer and Judi has her own home-based business as a graphic artist. Within their price range are a large loft in an up-and-coming neighborhood, a duplex apartment in a more established neighborhood, and moving to the suburbs a half-hour's train commute away from David's job in midtown Manhattan.

Both Judi and David sat down and together decided the factors that were important to them as a family. On their list their priorities—in no particular order—were:

Space
Schools for the Children
Neighbors
Cultural Activities
Entertainment
Cost of Food
Cost of Maintaining House
Career Advancement—Judi
Career Advancement—David
Safety of Neighborhood
Babysitters
Family Members
Community Services
Community Involvement
Roots
Transportation

Together Judi and David went through their list and assigned a weight to each factor. Influencing their feelings was the knowledge that wherever they moved, they intended it to be permanent, the place where their children would grow up, the place where they would put down solid family and community roots, socially and professionally. After discussing the factor weights together, their list looked like this:

Space ... 8
Schools for Children ... 9
Neighbors ... 7
Cultural Activities ... 5
Entertainment ... 4
Cost of Food ... 7
Cost of Maintaining House ... 8
Career Advancement—Judi ... 8
Career Advancement—David ... 8
Safety of Neighborhood ... 9
Babysitters ... 7
Family Members ... 3
Community Services ... 5
Community Involvement ... 6
Roots ... 7
Transportation ... 5

Since Judi and David's families lived in Ohio and Arizona, respectively, "Family Members" was given a "3" because, no matter where they moved, relatives would have to travel to visit them, anyway. While Judi and David love the proximity to theater and dance and other cultural/entertainment activities in New York, they realized that they rarely took full advantage of them, and gave these factors lower weights. "Safety of Neighborhood" and "Schools for the Children" rated high, as did the "Career Advancement" factors for both of them, who love their jobs and wish to continue to grow in professional and financial stature. "Transportation" rated a 5 because David could walk, take the subway or the commuter train to work, while Judi works at home.

Their next task was to set up three columns beside their factors representing their three possible choices: a spacious loft in a neighborhood that was beginning to be gentrified, with lots of young professionals like themselves moving in; a three-bedroom duplex with a small garden on a well-tended street in Greenwich Village, within walking distance of David's office; a suburban house with four bedrooms, garage, medium-size backyard, only a half-hour by train away from the city. Considering each choice one at a time, they assigned a number value for each factor, until their chart looked like this:

	Loft	Duplex	Suburban House
Space ... 8	5	6	7
Schools for the Children ... 9	4	8	9
Neighbors ... 7	7	8	6
Cultural Activities ... 5	8	9	4
Entertainment ... 4	8	9	3
Cost of Food ...7	6	6	10
Cost of Maintaining House ... 8	4	5	8
Career Advancement—Judi ...8	9	9	8
Career Advancement —David ... 8	9	9	6
Safety of Neighborhood ... 9	4	6	9
Babysitters ... 7	4	4	8
Family Members ... 3	3	3	2
Community Services ... 5	4	6	9
Community Involvement ... 6	7	7	5
Roots ... 7	7	7	6
Transportation ... 5	5	9	3

While Judi and David saw that in the suburbs the schools, availability of babysitters, safety factors, and community services were better, they also saw that their involvement, local services, and friends rated higher in Manhattan, which, while expensive, was still within their budget. Their next step was to multiply each factor's weight individually by the number they had assigned to each of their three choices.

After they finished, they added up the totals, which looked like this:

Loft	Duplex	Suburban House
662	750	982

Judi and David were surprised that the suburbs won out, but what surprised them the most was how far apart the totals were. They knew instantly that the loft—with its exciting but marginal neighborhood and services not entirely in place, was not for them. Besides, the loft itself would cost a lot of money to fix up to accommodate the needs of a growing family.

They also thought that it might be a good idea to examine the duplex vs. the suburbs a bit more closely, perhaps to go through the Easy Decisions process again with just the two choices to be considered. While they could proceed with buying the suburban house at this point, they would also have the choice of examining this new choice using the system, supplying additional factors that they might have forgotten the first time around. But even at this stage they had eliminated one choice, the loft, and felt good about that progress.

Using the system for shelter decisions extends past deciding whether to buy. Now that you've seen how Judi and David decided against the loft, you can use Easy Decisions to choose renting vs. buying, apartment vs. house, having a place of your own vs. moving in with friends or family, buying or renting a second or vacation home vs. saving that money for vacation . . . even whether to redecorate or renovate your existing home or apartment.

• NO-WIN DECISIONS •

Our next decision involves the workplace, the boss—and drugs, a social problem. While the example may seem extreme, it does point out how the system can be used to make ethical and business choices. We spend the majority of our waking time at work, and how happy or unhappy we are there colors our leisure time as well as our relationships with friends and family.

The system can be used to decide whether or not we're happy doing what we're doing and, if not, to discover what other work might be more important and satisfying to us. What kind of work to choose, where and with whom to work, political decisions made with co-workers at the office, whether to stay in the office or become our own bosses—all of these business-related decisions can be made using the Easy Decisions system.

You'll see that many of the considerations in this example are negative ones—no-win choices, if you will. That's for a reason. Often the choices we must make involve negative factors; not all decisions are made using only positive alternatives. Often these difficult decisions force us to choose the least offensive of several offensive paths. While it would be nice to choose among positive options, life doesn't always work that way. This is what Fred discovered when he came up against his unhappy business dilemma. Let's see how he handled it, using our system.

• A BUSINESS DILEMMA •

Fred works as a junior executive in the shipping division of a major manufacturing company. He was hired for the position by Walter, a friend from college who is manager of Fred's division. They've always gotten along and it's a good place to work. Fred's been there two years, and Walter has hinted at a promotion soon. As a result of his job, Fred has been able to save a little money and begin to think about settling down and finally marrying Lucy, his high school sweetheart. His responsibilities at work are increasing, and he finds his job challenging.

But lately something has been terribly wrong. Walter, normally outgoing and enthusiastic, has been increasingly jumpy and short tempered. He seems to go through mood swings—almost manic highs and brooding lows where he snaps at everyone around him—and business is beginning to suffer as a result. Fred has tried to ask him how he's feeling, inviting Walter for coffee after work. But Fred's getting nowhere—not only are his invitations turned down, but Walter seems to be almost paranoid. Sometimes at work he rambles on about "people out to get me," and has accused Fred of "spying" on him. His treatment of his other employees has gone downhill; a man who used to be friendly and a capable, sensitive manager has suddenly turned into a surly, angry boss who revels in undermining his subordinates' self-esteem. It's no longer a good place to work.

Fred is particularly worried, because a week ago he found out the reason for Walter's strange behavior. Staying late to finish a report, he noticed a light on in Walter's office. He was going to go inside, but what he saw made him stop: there was Walter, hunched over his desk, sniffing up what looked to be a sizable little heap of white powder. When he was finished, he looked furtively around his office, cleaned his desktop, then closed his briefcase. Fred, undetected, witnessed the whole thing. And, once he did, he was faced with a decision.

Fred went home that night and tried to sort out his thoughts. He knew he was facing a decision where both alternatives he was considering were painful, no matter what he did. On the one hand, he could ignore what he had seen, hope that Walter would snap out of his drug abuse problem, or, worse, put up with the increasingly terrible office atmosphere if Walter continued. On the other hand, he could confront Walter about his problem, advise him to get help, and try to make things better. Considering Walter's recent behavior, Fred doubted if his overtures of concern would be accepted. What's worse, Walter had hired him and, now that things had been going well for Fred, Walter could fire him. Just like that.

Fred decided to use the decision-making system to figure out what he should do. He knew that any decision he would make would be a risk, but he realized that to do nothing was a decision that might not be the best choice. Considering his situation, he wrote a list of factors that pertained to his work and Walter. They looked like this:

Work Atmosphere
Walter's Friendship
Own Finances
Another Job
Responsibility to Others
Ultimatum
Stay in Job

Violence
Moral Values

Fred had to consider many things: the possibility of losing his job, the loss of a (formerly) good friend. He's never been good at confrontation, and isn't sure if he can deliver an ultimatum. He's also afraid of violence from Walter, who has become very unpredictable lately. Fred considers himself a loyal friend, but he's not best-friend close with Walter, and at the same time he cares about others who, like him, have to labor in a demoralizing atmosphere. He likes his job, and is loathe to begin to look for another. He considers each factor, and gives the following weights:

Work Atmosphere ... 7
Walter's Friendship ... 4
Own Finances ... 8
Another Job ... 6
Responsibility to Others ... 6
Ultimatum ... 3
Stay in Job ... 9
Violence ... 4
Moral Values ... 9

Fred isn't sure what "Moral Values" really means, but it's an idea he feels is important in the situation, a good balance to purely practical considerations.

Maybe it's the voice of his mother in his ear, or the voice of his clergyman; it's intuitive, and he knows that it should figure somewhere on the list.

Next Fred makes his columns for possible options, and gives them numerical values according to what he thinks the consequences would be. The issue for him is not whether Walter will self-destruct or not, but whether or not he can save his job and do the best thing under the circumstances. What he sees when he is through surprises him:

	Do Nothing	Confront
Work Atmosphere ... 7	2	6
Walter's Friendship ... 4	5	3
Own Finances ... 8	8	4
Another Job ... 6	4	2
Responsibility to Others ... 6	2	8
Ultimatum ... 3	4	2
Stay in Job ... 9	3	3
Violence ... 4	4	7
Moral Values ... 9	2	10

Fred multiplies the factor weight by the value he's assigned for each decision possibility, then adds up the two columns for the total:

Do Nothing	Confront
207	297

Fred decides to confront Walter with what he has seen, to offer support and to see if it will make a difference. Perhaps it was the "Moral Values" question that clinched it; Fred just felt that to stand by silently not only would possibly make the situation deteriorate further, but it just wouldn't feel right to him.

He knows that he is risking a lot by confrontation. He knows his job may be on the line. But by going through the system in this no-win situation, Fred has discovered some positive things about himself— his sense of right and wrong—that he's never had to confront in himself before. This has given him a new measure of self-confidence, whatever the outcome. He decides to call a local drug-abuse counseling program and talk to an expert about what he should say before he talks to Walter in private. He knows that it will be tricky, but armed with some professional advice Fred knows that he might possibly be able to make a difference—for himself, for Walter, and for his co-workers.

Obviously, not all the decisions we have to make are easy ones. Often we are forced to deal with two or more alternatives, none of which are pleasant. It would be so much easier to wish them away, but life—like taxes—doesn't work that way. With our system it's possible to make the best-considered decision, even if the choice is between two negatives.

LIFE OR DEATH DECISIONS

Sometimes we have to confront very painful decisions that have powerful moral and ethical aspects to them. The system can also help where moral, as well as emotional and factual, dimensions are involved. Other people's values are irrelevant. What *is* important is *your* moral sense.

Our example here involves a wrenching life-or-death decision, but the system can also serve as a model for other soul-searching medical and moral choices where individual value systems can come into play: abortion, surrogate parenting, living wills, prenatal screening for birth defects, deciding whether to undergo certain kinds of cancer treatments, choices involving long-term quality of life.

When Amy and Peter first had to make their difficult choice, the Easy Decisions system enabled them to make their decision with less anguish. Here's what happened:

Amy's mother, Esther, was seventy-nine years old and had suffered a massive stroke. Esther was on life-support systems for eight weeks. The doctors said that there was no chance of recovery. Even if she survived, there had been catastrophic brain damage and she would be little more than a vegetable. The decision confronting Amy and Peter, her totally supportive husband, was whether to instruct the doctors to unplug the machines or to continue using heroic efforts to keep her alive.

On speaking to Amy eighteen months after her decision, I found that she and Peter had tried to consider their decision from every possible angle. They tried to think of everything. We decided together to reconstruct their decision in order to process it through our system, after the fact. Here is what Amy and Peter's final chart looked like:

	Turn Off Machines		Maintain Supports	
Pain to Esther ... −10	2	−20	3	−30
Possibility of Recovery ... 10	1	10	2	20
Morally Right ... 10	5	50	5	50
Personal Guilt ... −3	4	−12	2	−6
Rabbi's Advice ... 4	10	40	0	0
What Esther Would Have Wanted ... 8	7	56	0	0
Right to Die with Dignity ... 6	7	42	0	0
Emotional Damage to Family ... −4	3	−12	6	−24
What Children Will Think ... 3	3	9	6	18
Financial Implications ... −2	0	0	2	−4
Legal Restraints ... 4	0	0	0	0
Totals		**163**		**24**

A number of the factors as they were evaluated and computed revealed much about Amy and Peter's ordeal and what they were forced to confront. Having Esther avoid pain, and the possibility of recovery were of the highest importance to them. But they were incapable of judging whether either alternative would really accomplish those results. Consequently, these factors played virtually no part in the decision.

In the end these factors had the greatest influence on their decision as revealed by the system: their Rabbi's advice, their guess of what Esther would have wanted, and her right to die with dignity.

While many of the decisions we face during our lives are personal and based on individual value systems, the terrible choice confronted here by Amy and Peter was the most difficult of their lives. Other people might not have felt the same anguish. Some people may regard pulling the life supports simply as murder and profoundly immoral, while others may see no moral implications at all.

Amy and Peter had decided to ask the doctors to turn off the machines, and the doctors abided by their decision. But after Esther's death, they never felt confident that they had done the right thing. Going through the system eighteen months after the decision had actually been made gave them some comfort, because it reminded them how complicated the decision was to make. With so many conflicting emotional and moral issues involved in their choice, the Easy Decisions system helped Amy and Peter to sort out what facts and feelings they had been struggling with and reassured them about the rightness, by their own estimation, of their ultimate decision.

● LEARNING BY EXAMPLES ●

The examples presented in the previous sections describe very different kinds of decisions. Decisions based more on facts (which college has more of what you're looking for, which neighborhood to move into), decisions based on emotions (whether to get a divorce), decisions based on moral issues (whether to remove a loved one from life supports, how to deal with a troubled business associate), decisions made individually and together (whether to have a baby).

But each decision has elements of head and heart to consider, thought through by very different people in very different circumstances. In the same circumstances, your factors, considerations, and weights may be similar or very different, too.

Yet all these decisions have one thing in common: the Easy Decisions system was used as a guide to map out the future or to double-check the past. And, perhaps as important, the system offers a tool for self-discovery, the best guide to a better future.

• A FINAL WORD •

In the previous pages we've seen how our system has helped people to decide whether to move and take a new job, to decide which college to attend, whether or not to divorce, and to re-check a difficult life-and-death decision. These examples were picked specifically to illustrate how the system works.

We have to make decisions every day of our lives, some minor, some major. You may have different or similar decisions to make. Choosing a college. Deciding on a first job. Whether to buy or rent a house or apartment. Where to invest. Whether to have a child or another child. Whether to marry, live with someone, or stay single. Should your parents move in with you? Should you move in with your parents? Where to vacation. Whether to go into therapy and, if so, what kind of therapy to choose. Firing an employee. Falling in love.

In every decision we make in life there are many factors to consider. Some decisions are meant to be made selfishly; others require us to think about the impact of our actions on others. But no matter what the decision, it is important to recognize that, being human, we can never know *all* the facts.

That's why we must be confident of working with whatever factors we know are important to us, and that's what the system offers. We know that decisions can change, just as the people who make them change. Circumstances surrounding a decision can change, too. But with Easy Decisions you now have a way to tap into those aspects of your life that directly affect a decision.

As we've seen, there are decisions where either choice is a winner, and decisions where neither choice is a happy one. But it is crucial to recognize that, whatever the outcome, if you've used the system you have the knowledge that you have carefully considered what factors are important, have gone through a self-evaluation that is at the same time simple and revealing. You have the comfort of knowing that your decision was made, not haphazardly or in the heat of an emotional moment, but carefully and for the best.

Easy Decisions allows for you to make these decisions by yourself and with others. In the latter case, it can also give you an insight into those people who are important to you. By going through the system thoughtfully, you can also learn how to communicate more effectively with those you love, to learn more about them and yourself in the process.

Conquering our fears about making decisions is the best way we have to grow and change. By turning a former foe—decision making—into a friend, we have put our fears into perspective and let our true thoughts and needs shine through.

THE KEYS TO GOOD DECISION MAKING

You're now ready to use the system for whatever decisions you choose to make. When you do, keep in mind the following important points:

- You know more than you think you do.
- You can change your decision based on the factors you know to be important.
- You are allowed to make decisions on emotional and instinctual as well as factual criteria. Both the head and the heart have important things to say, if we just take the time to listen.
- You can go through the system as many times as you wish. Taking the time to double-check our moods, feelings, and factors is not a waste of time; rather, it builds even more confidence in our final choices.

- Keep your decision sheets. In them, you will have a record of your own changes, growth, and value systems. They will help you in making future decisions as well.
- There will always be decisions that are distasteful to make and uncomfortable to think through. The only error you can make is not to make those decisions at all, thereby giving up control over your life to others.
- Take as much time as you need. It is *your* decision, after all.
- No one factor is too trivial or too important to consider.
- Don't hesitate to involve loved ones in the system if your decision will affect them, but also keep in mind that sometimes their take on choices might be at odds with yours.
- *Trust yourself.* There are no truly bad decisions, just choices that haven't been thought through enough. If your choice displeases you, you can often make another. The planet, believe me, will not stop spinning. And you will have learned something you hadn't known before.
- Don't dwell on past "bad" decisions. It is the

easiest way to fall into the biggest Decision Trap of all—not making one in the first place. Look forward, not back. Use the system to recheck what happened. And go on from there with confidence.

That, after all, is what decision making is all about, and what the Easy Decisions system can do. You now have a user-friendly tool to chart your progress and take action. Take time to listen to your head and your heart. It's time to move forward. Good luck!

INTRODUCTION TO WORKSHEET SECTION

To get you started making easier decisions, here are some blank worksheets. The key to making the right decision is in your list of factors. Let's say you're thinking of a vacation, but aren't sure where you want to go. Under Factors, list (in no particular order) the things about a vacation that are important to you: fresh air, no crowds, cultural sights, cost involved, doing your own cooking, restaurants, theme park proximity, peace and quiet—whatever you choose.

When you have your list in the first column, then assign a Weight to each, from 1 (least important) to 10 (very important). Take your time . . . and add any other factors that may come to mind. (Keep in mind that these weights can also be negative numbers. A large negative number means that the factor is very important—but has negative consequences.)

Now you're ready for the next two (or more)

columns—Options. Say your first option is "Disney World." Put that at the head of the column. Your next might be "Seashore." Put that at the top of the second option column. If "Europe" is also an option, put that in a third column.

Starting with "Disney World," put a numerical Value from 1 to 10 opposite each of your factors—Restaurants, No Crowds, Cost, etc.—and do this for each of the options. (These values indicate—again on a scale of 1 to 10—just how well that particular option satisfies what you're looking for in that factor.)

When you're done filling in the comparative Value for all of the factors, get out your handy calculator and multiply each option value by the weight you gave to the corresponding factor, and put that result in the score column following each column of values.

All that's left to do is add up each of these "multiplied" columns. The option with the highest total shows you which decision you want to make. Of course you can change your mind, throw in new factors, rethink the weights you've assigned to the factors, etc. But when you're through, you should have a very good idea of the course of action that's best for you. You can use these worksheets or make some of your own, if you like. Remember—it's *your* system now!

Happy decision making—the easy way.

• THE EASY DECISIONS WORKSHEET •

	Option #1		Option #2	
Factor ... Weight (W)	Value (V)	W × V	Value (V)	W × V
1.				
2.				
3.				
4.				
5.				
6.				
7.				
8.				
9.				
etc.				

Totals

• THE EASY DECISIONS WORKSHEET •

	Option #1		Option #2	
Factor ...				
Weight (W)	Value (V)	W × V	Value (V)	W × V
1.				
2.				
3.				
4.				
5.				
6.				
7.				
8.				
9.				
etc.				

Totals

● ABOUT THE AUTHOR ●

Mary Alice Kellogg is a former associate editor for *Newsweek*, senior editor of *Parade* and on-air correspondent for WCBS-TV in New York. Her writing appears regularly in many national publications, among them *Travel & Leisure, Gentlemen's Quarterly, Glamour, Harper's Bazaar, Redbook* and *Bride's*.

An editorial consultant and lecturer on media and career issues, she has made frequent appearances on local and national television. Her previous book, *Fast Track*, was one of the first to look at the effects of the baby boom generation on American life. She lives in New York and Sag Harbor, Long Island.

• AUTHOR'S NOTE •

How has *Hard Choices, Easy Decisions* worked for you? As I meet people who have used the system, I'm continually amazed by the variety of situations—some serious, some screwball —in which the system has been helpful.

Feedback is very important in decision making, and authors are no exception. If you've used the system and have a decision you'd like to share, I'd like to hear about it; perhaps some of them will be included in a future book on the subject. Send your stories to the author at the following address, and thank you.

Mary Alice Kellogg
℅ First Run Features
153 Waverly Place
New York, New York 10014